Original title:
Sliced into the Soul

Copyright © 2025 Creative Arts Management OÜ
All rights reserved.

Author: Jude Lancaster
ISBN HARDBACK: 978-1-80586-285-7
ISBN PAPERBACK: 978-1-80586-757-9

## Echoes of the Unhealed

In the mirror, I see my fries,
Wonder where the ketchup lies.
Thoughts are like popcorn, they pop,
But I seem to have dropped the mop.

Hearts go bump in a funny way,
Like a cat when it tries to play.
We laugh at the ghosts of our dreams,
Yet the toaster still burns at our schemes.

## **Sands of Forgotten Time**

Time slips like sand through my hand,
Like a poorly planned sleight of hand.
Each grain tells a joke or a tale,
But my watch seems to always fail.

I dance like a fool in the sun,
Thinking a nap is just too much fun.
The clock chuckles at my slow pace,
Yet here I am, lost in this race.

## Breaths of Fragility

Life's a souffle, so light and grand,
Watch me fumble with fork and hand.
The laughs wrap around like a breeze,
While I trip over unexpected cheese.

Each giggle's a bubble that floats,
Every hiccup brings laughter in boats.
I juggle my thoughts with pies in the sky,
Two misses so far, and I'm just that guy.

## The Weight of the Unexpressed

Words piled up like laundry on chairs,
Waiting for someone who cares.
I balled up my angst in a sock,
While pondering the ticking of the clock.

Giggles linger in the unspoken,
Like a vow that was only broken.
I fling out my thoughts like confetti bright,
Hoping they land and take flight tonight.

## Layers of the Unspoken

Beneath my skin, there's chatter,

Thoughts parade, all that's the matter.

Sandwich shop with no ingredients,

What a feast of nonsense and lenience.

Dreams stack high like a pancake,

Each layer hides just one mistake.

Hope they don't flop on my plate,

Or folks will laugh, 'What a fate!'

Onions peel my deeper woes,

Cream cheese spreads on all that grows.

A bagel twist of what I feel,

Yet my truth is a thin layer, surreal.

**The Cost of Clarity**

Woke up today with vision clear,

But tripped on thoughts that weren't so dear.

The price of insight's quite absurd,

Thoughts cost a dime, silence a bird.

Buy two truths, get one lie free,

Exchange some clarity for a cup of tea.

I laughed at my wallet's empty grin,

Turns out wisdom's a joke too thin.

Wisdom wears mismatched socks,

Clueless sheep stuck in paradox.

Clarity says, 'Do heed my call,'

So why did I just trip and fall?

## Echoes of Absence

There's a party in the room I'm missing,

Dancing shadows, bottles glistening.

I linger near the doorframe, shy,

While echoes of laughter drift on by.

Forgot to RSVP to my own event,

The punchline's here, yet I'm absent.

Balloons float with a cheerful grin,

But my inner clown forgot to begin.

They say laughter fills the gaps of space,

Yet here I am, a ghostly face.

My sense of humor lost and found,

In every silence, another sound.

## **Faint Marks of Existence**

In the morning light, I take a peek,

Life's faint marks leave me quite weak.

Like a sketch in a dusty book,

I nod at shadows, oh, how they crook.

Like toast that burnt on the one side,

Faint traces of joy that I can't abide.

I'm the comma in a giant pause,

A footnote with no greater cause.

Existence wears a silly hat,

Walking around like an awkward cat.

With wobbly steps on this tightrope,

Faint marks of existence and a lost hope.

## **The Deep Cut of Longing**

A knife so sharp, yet dull with dread,
It might just slice my thoughts instead.
With every laugh, a little bleed,
Who knew longing could be this absurdly freed?

I search for comfort in a pie,
But it just rolls away, oh my!
A craving for joy, a tongue in cheek,
My heart's a joke, but it still feels weak.

## **Threads of Emotion Unraveled**

These threads I pull, why do they tangle?
Like spaghetti nights when hunger's a dangle.
I trip on feelings, pull a thread too tight,
It unravels my sanity, but what a silly sight!

A sweater knitted from hopes and dreams,
Turns into a pun, bursting at the seams.
With stitches of laughter, I patch the low,
Yet it falls apart, like jokes in a show.

## **Veins of Dawn and Dusk**

Morning light shoots straight through the veins,
While evening gloom spills out the pains.
I sip my coffee and watch it swirl,
Expecting humor in the drama's whirl.

Butterflies sting as day folds to night,
Each moment's a laugh in this odd little fight.
I dance with shadows, let silliness flow,
With sunrise sprinkles and moonbeam glow.

## Shadows Cast on Inner Light

My shadows giggle while they tease,
They tickle the thoughts that don't quite please.
What a sight to see, a shadow's delight,
Making me chuckle, oh what a night!

Inner light flickers like a bulb on a prank,
Casting odd shapes in my emotional bank.
Laughter erupts as shadows engage,
In this hilarious dance, I'm the center stage.

## **Splintered Thoughts**

A quirk of fate, my mind's a mess,
A jigsaw puzzle, always a guess.
Laughter's the glue that holds it tight,
In chaos, I dance, ready to ignite.

Ideas pop like balloons in the air,
Each one a wild, whimsical flair.
I trip on the thoughts, they giggle and squeal,
Who knew my brain could have such a reel?

Cracks in my logic, they joke and tease,
Witty banter comes with such ease.
I chuckle at scars that mark my ride,
A silly parade where nonsense can glide.

# Wounds of the Mind

Oh, the blunders that stumble and fall,
Like clowns in a circus that trip down the hall.
My brain's a carnival, tangled and bright,
Where laughter weaves in, igniting the night.

Every mishap, a punchline to share,
I can't keep a secret, it's all out there.
Eureka! I shout as I lose the plot,
But in this chaos, I've found quite a lot.

Jokes turn my scars into glittering dreams,
Life's comedic as it merrily seems.
With wounds of the mind, I'll dance and I'll sing,
For laughter's the joy that each moment brings.

## Fragments of Essence

Tiny pieces litter my headspace wide,
Like confetti tossed on a tear-stained ride.
Each fragment a story, a giggle or two,
That glitter in shadows, like morning dew.

I trip over memories, scattered and spry,
They twirl in the air like a butterfly.
With snickers and snorts, they all come alive,
In the chaos of bits, my spirits thrive.

Segments of wisdom, misfit and rare,
Teaching me humor in every affair.
From nonsense to wisdom, I'll weave my tale,
In silliness wrapped, I shall never fail.

## **Shadows of Vulnerability**

In shadows that dance like they own the show,
I strut with my quirks, taking it slow.
With every misstep, I find a delight,
As humor embraces my awkward plight.

These shadows may whisper and tease at the past,
But laughter's the sunshine, it's built to last.
Each stumble, a joke that I gladly recite,
In the theater of fools, I find my light.

Vulnerability prances, a comical sight,
It's all part of life, a colorful flight.
So here's to the flaws that make us so whole,
In the tapestry of laughter, I've found my role.

## Raw and Unfiltered

In a world of ketchup dreams,
Where mustard reigns supreme,
I bite into a juicy scheme,
And laugh at my own meme.

Fridge raiders in the night,
Conspiring with the light,
A dance with pickles bright,
We feast until the light.

Spatulas are our swords,
Pancakes sing in chords,
Maple syrup hoards,
While laughter's never bored.

So join this funny feast,
As crumbs reveal the beast,
In every bite, a jest,
Unfiltered, we are blessed.

**Eclipsed by Emotion**

A sandwich stacked too high,
With thoughts I can't deny,
Mustard pools just like my sigh,
Tomato's red, oh my, oh my!

I trip on butter's slick delight,
As cookies argue who's more right,
In this snack attack, no end in sight,
Giggles burst, a funny fright!

Carrots clash in crunchy wars,
With celery that just adores,
To make a salad, hear the roars,
Of laughter echoing in the stores.

So when I'm feeling blue,
I grab a bite or two,
In every chew, a skewed view,
Funny munching, just for you.

## The Undercurrent of Pain

An onion's tear, oh what a flair,
Chopping's never quite so fair,
As garlic whispers, 'Let's prepare!'
My cooking skills? A wild affair.

Chili burns with spicy prose,
While laughter in the kitchen grows,
Dancing vegetables strike a pose,
In this funny chaos that nobody knows.

Mistakes served with a side of grace,
A burned roast in a smoky space,
"Let's just order!" I embrace,
In food, we find our funny place.

So here's to every odd delight,
To cooking fails that bring us light,
In culinary battles, day and night,
Find joy, and keep your heart in sight!

## Labyrinth of Memory

In the pantry, ghosts arise,
Of cookies lost 'neath big surprise,
Prunes declare they're wise to rise,
In this maze of sneaky pies.

Spaghetti tangles with a twist,
As garlic bread gets quite the mist,
A fork's a maze, a funny gist,
In every bite, I can't resist.

Broccoli wears a funny crown,
In veggie courts, it won't back down,
Cauliflower's the joker's gown,
In laughter's feast, we'll never frown.

So dive into this edible tale,
Where munch and crunch will never pale,
In humor's kitchen, we set sail,
With every flavor, we prevail.

## The Space Where Shadows Lie

In corners dark where secrets dwell,
A sock, a shoe, a hidden bell.
With laughter echoing through the night,
We chase the phantoms out of sight.

A ghost may tap upon my door,
Offering me a sweet encore.
But as I dance with wobbly grace,
I trip and fall, right on my face.

The shadows giggle, what a sight!
They whisper tales of silly fright.
Yet in this gloom, I see the fun,
For every night must have its run.

When sunlight peeks to end the game,
The laughter lingers, always same.
We'll meet again when night is bold,
In spaces where the shadows hold.

## Embers of Past Affliction

Burnt toast and coffee, morning cheer,
The recipe of yesteryear.
With smudged regrets upon the plate,
I laugh and sip the crumbs of fate.

A fire alarm blares overhead,
I dance around, still half in bed.
The embers of my breakfast woe,
Bring bittersweet laughs, it's how we grow.

With every toast that turns to ash,
I find a way to make a splash.
The kitchen's chaos brings delight,
As I create my burnt-up bite.

Yet through the smoke and stifled sound,
The warmth of laughter can be found.
For even in mishaps, life's a show,
It's the ember's glow that steals the show.

## Prism of Broken Trust

A friendship's shard upon the floor,
With glitter scattered, ever more.
We chuckle at the ways we've bent,
In colors bright, our lives are spent.

Promises made with rainbow glee,
Yet sometimes life plays tricks on me.
An errant joke spills from my lips,
We find ourselves on funny trips.

With shadows cast from glassy seams,
We make our way through silly dreams.
A prism shows the fractures clear,
Yet laughter's light is always near.

In broken trust, a spark ignites,
We stumble on through quirky nights.
For in the cracks, we find our place,
In silly smiles and warm embrace.

## The Gentle Pull of Hidden Grief

A teddy bear, with fur so worn,
Holds secrets of the heart, forlorn.
Yet in its hug, a funny twist,
It teases sorrow with a tryst.

Behind the smile, a kernel hides,
Life's ups and downs like roller rides.
A chuckle bursts through heavy sighs,
So even grief can wear disguise.

Each tear that spills, a dance of flair,
As laughter mingles with despair.
The gentle pull of what we feel,
Turns pain to joy, it's quite the deal.

So raise a glass to what we share,
In laughing fits, we strip the bare.
For hidden grief can spin a tale,
Of joy and laughter to prevail.

## **The Soul's Quiet Echo Chamber**

In a room where laughter bounces,
Echoes of joy just take their chances.
A joke misplaced, a giggle's flight,
The shadows dance into the night.

Bouncing thoughts, all out of tune,
A cat that sings a merry croon.
The whispers of a chocolate cake,
Make hearts giggle, and stomachs ache.

Reflections swim in a strange glass sea,
Funny faces stare back at me.
The soul clumsily trips and falls,
Into a laughter that never stalls.

So chuckle more, with all your might,
Embrace the chaos, it feels so right.
In this chamber, joy's the call,
Echoes of laughter, we share it all.

## Reflections in a Fractured Mirror

In a mirror cracked, my face awry,
One eye winks, the other can't lie.
I trip on smiles, in silly glee,
Who knew reflections could play with me?

Each shard reflects a different tale,
A prince, a frog, a goofy snail.
As I pose for my portrait grand,
My hair's an art form, quite unplanned.

A giggle lurks in every line,
As I squint at the view, divine.
Shattered glass shows an odd parade,
Of fancy dreams that I once made.

So let's toast to this bubbly fun,
In laughter's web, we're all spun.
With every glance, nothing's quite core,
In fractured worlds, we'll still explore.

## **The Weight of Forgotten Dreams**

I dreamed of flying, what a big thought,
But now I'm grounded by what I forgot.
A balloon that drifted, way up high,
Now sits in the corner and wonders why.

Weighty dreams in a suitcase, packed,
A comedy show that fate hijacked.
They bounce around in a jester's bow,
I trip over wishes, as they somehow grow.

In a tangle of hopes and old stuffed bears,
Lies a treasure trove of forgotten snares.
They wait for laughter, a playful tease,
Who needs a map when you've got cheese?

So grab those dreams, take them for a ride,
In a world where laughter won't ever hide.
Dance with the weight of what once seemed,
Funny how life can mend what's dreamed.

## Stitches in Time's Tattered Quilt

With needle and thread, I patch my tale,
Stitches that wiggle, some wiggle and flail.
Each square a memory, some bright, some odd,
A quilt of giggles that I nod, applaud.

In time's tattered weave, I find a sock,
Stitched with humor, it's quite the rock.
A mismatched pair, oh what a sight,
Recalling adventures that feel so right.

Every thread tells a story, you see,
Of puppies, parties, and wild jubilee.
In stitches, laughter begins to unfold,
The fabric of life, both warm and bold.

So let's gather round this patchwork charm,
Embrace the quirkiness, it keeps us warm.
In time's quilted embrace, we find the loot,
A funny life sewn in each little root.

## The Silence Within

In the quiet, I hear a sneeze,
A tickle in my memories' breeze.
They whisper secrets, but I just laugh,
Empty spaces, a ghostly gaffe.

A sock rolls by, it knows the score,
It once had company, now it's sore.
It snickers as it tells its tale,
Of mismatched pairs that always fail.

I sip my tea, it spills with grace,
Caught in the silence, it starts to race.
Laughter floats on the vapor trails,
An echo of joy, like a hundred sprails.

So here I sit, with ghosts galore,
Sharing old jokes, I can't ignore.
In this silence, I find my cheer,
Even shadows can crack a beer.

## Ghosts of the Past

Old photographs with funny hair,
Laughing faces caught in despair.
They shimmy and shake in dusty frames,
Telling tales with silly names.

Each ghost winks like it knows a prank,
A dance of memories, all in a tank.
They tickle my heart, those fleecy dreams,
And burst with laughter at life's extremes.

There's Grandma's wig, on a cat's big head,
That feline strutted until it spread.
The laughter echoes in rooms of lore,
Perhaps there's more, or maybe just four.

And as I chuckle at that fateful night,
When my brothers danced and just took flight,
Ghosts flutter by, with a meaningful cheer,
All past troubles seem far, yet near!

## Chiseled by Experience

With every laugh line deepening now,
I've carved my stories, but I'll take a bow.
For every slip that made me fall,
A statue made of giggles stands tall.

They chiseled away with the finest jest,
In each mishap, I simply invest.
I've learned to trip while stealing a glance,
Who knew a stumble could start a dance?

With friends beside me, we whip and sway,
Memory clay molds us as we play.
Each bruise a badge of humor's grace,
A montage of smiles etched on my face.

Show me your scars, I'll show you mine,
Let's trade our tales, let's intertwine.
Chiseled memories guide the way,
In our gallery of laughter, we'll stay.

## Hearts in Tidal Flow

In oceans deep, my heart does float,
Tangled in laughter, I choose to gloat.
The waves, they tickle and tease my soul,
Surfing on froth, I'm out of control.

Waves crash in, creating a mess,
Salty spray, and oh, the distress!
But oh, how I love this watery plight,
Dancing with dolphins, a comical sight.

As tides pull back, I may feel blue,
But seaweed smiles, as if it knew.
A sea of laughter, a buoyant call,
In this tidal flow, we rise and fall.

So hold on tight to the beach of dreams,
For the moon's a joker, or so it seems.
He pulls at our hearts in ebb and crest,
In waves of humor, we find our jest.

## Ribbons of Wounds and Wishes

My heart's a piñata, all tied up with bows,
Each hit that I take, just a slap and a prose.
With wishes like confetti that scatter and swirl,
I laugh at the chaos, oh what a grand twirl!

Strains of my laughter mix with the tears,
Like clowns at a party, facing all fears.
Each ribbon unraveled tells stories so bright,
Of wounds turned to jokes in the soft, glimmering light.

## **A Tear in the Fabric of Being**

In the fabric of life, a stitch found its way,
Like a sock with a hole, driving neatness away.
I dance with the chaos, embrace every snag,
And wear my odd patterns like a colorful rag!

A tear in my psyche, a quirk in the seam,
A fabric of laughter, a fabric of dream.
With patches of folly sewn snug with a grin,
I twirl in the sunlight, let the oddness begin!

## **Photographs of Unspoken Pain**

Snapshots of giggles, where silence has crept,
A wink and a nod, and I quietly wept.
These photographs hidden, they chuckle and tease,
Like mimes in the park, bringing me to my knees.

The lens caught the fumbles, the slips on the floor,
An unspoken pain, oh, who could ask for more?
Each click of the shutter reveals the absurd,
In laughter, we linger, it's all quite unheard!

## Wounds that Blossom in the Dark

In shadows they flourish, these blooms of despair,
With petals of giggles, floating in air.
A wound that once stung now flutters with grace,
Like daisies in moonlight, oh what a strange place!

They whisper and chuckle, these flowers of woe,
Their roots twist in laughter, putting on a show.
With every new petal that tickles the night,
I chuckle at sorrow; it all feels just right!

## Shattered Reflections

In mirrors cracked, my face does dance,
A lopsided grin, a silly glance.
I pose and pout, a comic show,
But look too close, and oh, the woe!

A whisker here, a smudge of pie,
Who knew my hair could defy the sky?
I laugh at flaws, my winsome fate,
Each shard a joke, oh how I've great!

Prancing like a jester, wild and free,
With each reflection, it's just me.
Broken bits can make me smile,
A comedy of errors, every while!

So catch my eye and share a grin,
In this funhouse, I'm bound to win.
With laughter echoing through the hall,
Come join the jest, and let's stand tall!

**Beneath the Surface**

In puddles deep, I spot a frog,
With bulging eyes, and belly log.
He hops and splashes, what a sight,
Ribbit-ting jokes, he's got it right!

Diving down, there's more in store,
At bottom's end, I find a chore.
A fish in glasses reads a book,
While turtles stare, of course, they look!

Bubbles rise with silly tunes,
Dancing with the sun and moons.
Who knew the world beneath could tease?
With tales of laughter that never cease!

So let's take a plunge, splash in fun,
With creatures wacky, we'll surely run.
We'll giggle deep, in waters free,
As life's a jest, just come and see!

**Carved Secrets**

On wooden beams, my secrets lay,
Like squirrels hoarding nuts, they stay.
Carved with glee, a heart, a name,
But mostly jokes, all in the frame!

A turtleneck carved, with bows and flair,
Jokes etched in bark, stories rare.
"Oh, how I spent a silly night!"
Whittled words make the laughter light!

Each knot a giggle, each grain a song,
In tree-tales where the pranks belong.
From roots to tip, let humor grow,
A life so carved, and don't you know?

So if you find a tree so wise,
With scribbled secrets, no surprise.
Just read the laughter, join the cheer,
In wooden whispers, jokes draw near!

## Veins of Unspoken Truth

Beneath my skin, absurdities dwell,
Like secret notes in a flowery well.
Pulsing with quirks, my heart does beat,
A rhythm funny, not quite discreet!

Like spaghetti tangled in a twist,
My thoughts run wild, impossible to list.
But every jolt, a chuckle finds,
As silly ponderings free our minds!

With every pulse, a quirky jest,
Unveiling mysteries, do your best!
Dancing veins that bubble and swirl,
A comedy of life, let laughter unfurl!

So peek inside these veins of mine,
Where giggles bloom like starry shine.
In this crazy heart, we play and jest,
A truth so funny, we are truly blessed!

**Threads Unraveled**

In the weavings of my mind, oh dear,
Lurks a sock with quite a tear.
It dances with a playful leap,
While I just sit here counting sheep.

My thoughts are like spaghetti strands,
Tangled up in awkward hands.
I trip over my own clever schemes,
Like chasing after winter dreams.

Sometimes I laugh, sometimes I cry,
As mismatched moments fly on by.
The fabric of my day is bright,
Stitched with quirks and pure delight.

A jester's cap upon my head,
With colors that can't be misread.
The unraveling brings me glee,
In a world of lively jubilee.

## Shades of Yearning

I yearn for snacks both sweet and bold,
Like chocolate dreams wrapped in gold.
The fridge, it whispers late at night,
With leftovers that seem just right.

My heart is like a pizza pie,
So many toppings, oh my, oh my!
A pinch of love, a dash of spice,
Just one more slice would be so nice!

Yet here I sit, counting my cash,
Wishing for a food love splash.
The shades of craving paint my world,
As my culinary flags unfurl.

With every craving, laughter grows,
I dream of feasts like summer shows.
In all this yearning, I shall find,
A happy plate, a joyful mind.

# The Quiet Rupture

A hush descends when I misstep,
The quiet break of my own rep.
A biscuit crumbles, sound so loud,
I laugh aloud, feel like a shroud.

The coffee spills, a dark explosion,
Creating quite the caffeinated commotion.
I giggle in this kitchen mess,
Where perfect moments feel less, not less!

I trip on my own two left feet,
A comic scene, so rough, not sweet.
But each blunder brings a grin,
In chaos, there's a dance within.

The quiet ruptures keep me sane,
Each little fail, a funny game.
Inside this life, both bright and funny,
I find my joy in the not-so-runny.

## Tapestry of Tears

My heart's a quilt, frayed and tattered,
Stitched with laughter, sometimes scattered.
Each patch a tale, a silly blunder,
I laugh till I cry, then hear the thunder.

Stitches pull tight, and some unravel,
I dance to the beat of a comical travel.
Each thread a smile, a chuckle spun,
In this tapestry, mischief's never done.

But oh, the knots, they tease my scheme,
With every tug, I'm lost in a dream.
Tears of joy thread through the seams,
A masterpiece born from quirky themes.

So here's to frays and joyful seams,
Life's just a patchwork of giggling dreams.
When the fabric's loose, it's a riotous scroll,
In laughter, I find the patch for my soul.

**Descent into Stillness**

In hush of the night, I'm too awake,
Whispers of silence, like a big mistake.
The clock's my enemy, ticks like a clown,
In stillness, I ponder why I don't frown.

Thoughts dive in silence, doing the twist,
They bubble and burst, like a comedian's list.
Falling through stillness, it's a funny show,
As my brain does somersaults, in a quiet flow.

Reflection's a mirror that giggles back,
With every thought, there's a comic crack.
Quiet's a jester, dancing alone,
While I sit in silence, feeling like a drone.

Yet in this stillness, jokes take flight,
Wave after wave, I'm tickled outright.
In the descent, laughter's the goal,
As I tumble through layers of my own soul.

## The Heart's Labyrinth

My heart's a maze, leads to nowhere,
With twists and turns, I laugh in despair.
Each corner I turn, a prankster awaits,
Playing hide and seek behind closed gates.

Lost in the loops, my heart's fine art,
Elusive love snickers, never to part.
Echoes of laughter fill every hall,
Where joy is the king, and heartbreak's small.

In shadows lurk jests, both clever and silly,
Each route I take, feels oddly frilly.
I dance with ghosts from moments past,
In this funny heart, shadows are cast.

So wander I will, with humor so bright,
In laughter's embrace, I feel so light.
For in this labyrinth, not all is toll,
A heart of giggles is an endless scroll.

## Canvas of Cracks

My canvas is wild, with many a crack,
Colors collide, and laughter's the knack.
Every drip of paint tells a tale of glee,
Where joy splatters bright, unrestrained and free.

Splashes of humor, some serious stains,
Dancing on edges, where nonsense reigns.
Cracks are the pathways for jokes to flow,
In this art of life, let the chaos show.

With brush in hand, I tickle dark hues,
Making the sad shades wear vibrant shoes.
Each brushstroke a giggle, each line takes flight,
On this canvas of cracks, all feels just right.

So here's to the mess, the laughter it brings,
In every imperfection, my heart always sings.
For on this canvas, life's a playful stroll,
And cracks are just windows to the buried soul.

## **Portraits of the Unshed Tear**

In the frame of a smile, a tear takes a bow,
A portrait of laughter, but who made it wow?
With brushes of joy, we daub on the paint,
Yet underneath grins, lies a cheeky complaint.

The canvas of life, a curious sight,
Splashes of humor take flight in the night.
Each strokes a joke that we share with a wink,
But deep in our hearts, we secretly think.

A masterpiece crafted with giggles and sighs,
Each droplet a treasure that never quite dries.
As colors collide like a wild game of darts,
We laugh at the tears that live in our hearts.

So here's to the portraits of joy turned to jest,
With each brush of humor, we're truly blessed.
In galleries bright where the giggles blend clear,
Life's canvas keeps showing us laughter and cheer.

## Puzzle Pieces of the Heart's Wound

A jigsaw of feelings, all scattered around,
Searching for pieces that simply confound.
With edges so sharp, they poke and they prod,
Yet fitting them in feels rather like a fraud.

Oh, what a game with no clear winning line,
The pieces are wrinkled, a real funny design.
Some corner is missing, another's upside down,
Yet we chuckle and glue, while we wear a frown.

Each section a story that's partly absurd,
Connecting the laughter, oh, how we've blurred!
When pieces collide, oh what a surprise,
A heart that once struggled now dances and flies.

So gather your puzzles, let's play with a grin,
For life's weird connections are where we begin.
In laughter we find that the wounds can be healed,
With humor's tight grip, the pain is concealed.

## A Glimpse Through the Veil of Emotion

Behind the curtain, emotions peek through,
With giggles and snorts, they bid us adieu.
The veil flutters softly, it's quite the charade,
Winking and bursting like jesters parade.

A tickle of sadness, a splash of delight,
When laughter takes flight, you can feel it ignite.
The glances exchanged, a mischief-filled game,
With bubbles of joy that put sorrow to shame.

From whispers of worry to hiccups of glee,
There's magic in moments that coax us to see.
So let's lift the veil with a contagious cheer,
Where humor's a beacon in gloom's atmosphere.

In this playful dance, emotions take flight,
A glimpse of the heart, surprisingly bright.
Let's chuckle at fears that once held us tight,
Through laughter, we find that it all feels just right.

**Tendrils of Memory and Loss**

Memory flitters like a feather in breeze,
Tickling the mind, bringing giggles with ease.
Tendrils of laughter entwine with the past,
A mix of the sweet with the bittersweet cast.

So here's to the moments that slip through our hands,
Like sand through an hourglass, as humor expands.
We chuckle at endings, they're starts in disguise,
For loss wears a grin, when we open our eyes.

With each little memory, a riddle unfolds,
As we laugh at our stories, both fresh and old.
The echoes of voices that tickle the heart,
Keep reminding us even the hurt is an art.

So tend to those memories, let laughter plant seeds,
In gardens of heartache, their humor now leads.
For every lost moment is also a chance,
To dance with the past, in a whimsical prance.

## Landscapes of the Unwound

In the garden of my brain, weeds do grow,
Every thought a bouncy ball, off they go.
Dancing flowers, talking trees in a mess,
All my plans have found their way to distress.

The sun is shining, but ducks wear shades,
Giggles echo where sanity fades.
My thoughts are like cats, they scatter and play,
Chasing thoughts, I hope they won't stray.

Clouds wearing socks, rain giving high-fives,
I've questioned if my humor still thrives.
A parade of socks rolls down my street,
Each one leaving me with mismatched feet.

Yet in this chaos, laughter I find,
A whimsical parade of the wayward mind.
With every chuckle, I gather my grace,
In the landscapes where unwinding takes place.

## **Heartstrings Untangled**

Strings from my heart, oh what a knot,
Each one a tale, or a prank, like it or not.
In the circus of feelings, I'm a clown, you see,
Juggling emotions, oh where will they be?

A bank of lost socks, my love life spills,
Chasing romance like it's found in drills.
Cupid with hiccups, shoots arrows wonky,
Love letters laugh at my failures so funky.

Rippling giggles float on the breeze,
A heart that dances with whimsical ease.
Tangled in joy, where laughter ignites,
Unraveling love in the oddest of bites.

Yet through the tangle, oh what a sight,
To find in this mess, laughter feels right.
Rescue me from being too serious, please,
My heartstrings belong to the jester's tease.

## **Reflections of a Fractured Mind**

A mirror cracked, what do I see,
Reflections of me, and a monkey in a tree.
Jumpsuits and polka dots, fashion so loud,
Every thought's a balloon, floating like a cloud.

Riddles of laughter bounce off the walls,
Each echo a joke, as the jester calls.
I trip on my brain, it's a slip and a slide,
In the funhouse of thoughts, there's nowhere to hide.

Maybe I'm a puzzle, missing some pieces,
The laughter within often just increases.
When thoughts get wacky, I play hide and seek,
Fractured reflections, but the humor's unique.

So I dance with my chaos, a comical twirl,
In a mind so quirky, let the laughter unfurl.
What's lost in the cracks can be found in delight,
A world where absurdity dances in light.

## Cracks in the Armor

My armor's a costume, a knight gone absurd,
With dents and with dings, it's laughter preferred.
As I gallop through life, jingles my chain,
In a world filled with whimsy, no need for the pain.

Every crack tells a story, oh what a plot,
Of falling flat on my face, and hitting a spot.
The sword's merely foam, in my playful fight,
Chasing dragons of doubt, with my shield made of light.

A treasure map leads to silliness bold,
In the land of the quirky, adventures unfold.
Armed with a grin and a heart full of jest,
With cracks in my armor, I feel truly blessed.

So here's to the laughter, the joy in the fray,
In this fun-loving battle, I'm here to stay.
For each crease is a smile, each dent a surprise,
Cracks in the armor are where humor lies.

## The Texture of Mourning

A banana peel on a serious day,
Slips and slides, it leads me astray.
My heart wears a frown, like a clown at the fair,
Juggling grief with a goofy flair.

When socks lost in dryers turn into a fight,
I mourn for the pairs that vanished from sight.
Each tear that I shed, like a drip of sweet brine,
Turns sorrow to giggles, it's my funny line.

Old photos tucked in a dusty old chest,
Reveal me in wigs, oh, guess who's the jest?
Mourning's just laughter wearing a cloak,
A pun on my heart, it's a jesting poke.

So bring on the comfort, the laughter we crave,
In the oddest of moments, our sorrows behave.
For mourning, you see, can take on a grin,
With joy in our hearts, let the fun times begin.

## Petals on Concrete

In a city of cheese, I walk with a sprout,
Blooms of pink petals that scream and shout.
They land on the pavement, a brave little dance,
Each step's a mix of clumsy romance.

Concrete is tough, and my feet go slap,
Petals laugh loudly, like friends in a gap.
"Why're you so serious?" they chirp with delight,
As I trip on my thoughts in the morning light.

A ladybug joins in, with a tiny top hat,
"Dance like it's fun!" it insists with a pat.
I twirl through the chaos, a sight to behold,
Petals and laughter, a story retold.

So let's carpet the streets with petals galore,
And chuckle at life as it opens each door.
For joy's in the cracks where the soft petals lie,
On concrete I laugh, let my spirit fly.

**The Fragrance of Farewell**

A whiff of old cheese as I wave goodbye,
It dances like skunks in the smoky sky.
Farewell whispers sweetly, like onions at dawn,
With laughter and tears, it moves us along.

Wrapped in a gift of a quirky perfume,
Each scent tells a story, each whiff goes boom!
Farewell isn't sad, it's a chance to eat pie,
With humor as seasoning, we'll all reach the sky.

The door closes softly, but a window ajar,
Invites in the winks from a nearby star.
I load up my bags with a giggle and grin,
Saying 'until next time,' let the fun times begin.

So come, take a whiff of the jokes that we share,
A fragrance of laughter is wafting in air.
Farewell is a scent that we'll carry with glee,
As we joke about life, just you wait and see.

**Crumbling Facades**

Behind all these smiles, I wear a facade,
Like a clown on the run from a bad masquerade.
Brick walls in my laugh with a hint of despair,
Yet dance is the trick, and I'm light as air.

Laughter erupts like popcorn in heat,
A facade comes crashing—oh, aren't we neat?
In the cracks of my sorrow, a punchline will bloom,
As I juggle my troubles, making space in the room.

A funny old hat sits atop of my head,
Each wobble a whisper, making sense of the dread.
Crumbling as I giggle, the walls start to sway,
With each silly moment, a new light of day.

So let's smooth our facades with a tickle of cheer,
For life's one big joke, let's make it quite clear!
Crumbling is fine, when you laugh on the fall,
In this comedy act, we can conquer it all.

## Beneath the Veil of Grace

I wore a smile, oh so wide,
But inside my heart, I tried to hide.
Like a jester in a sad parade,
With echoes of laughter, still afraid.

The world watched me dance, a bold charade,
While confetti of kindness slowly frayed.
With each joyful twirl, I spun my tale,
But behind the laughter, I'd sometimes pale.

Juggling my woes like a clown in boots,
Flinging pies of joy in comical suits.
Yet, when the curtain finally drew close,
I bowed to the audience, they never chose.

Lessons in giggles, love tightly laced,
Underneath it all, a funny grace.
In the circus of life, I take off the mask,
Finding humor in sorrow, a joy to unmask.

## The Anatomy of Heartache

In the lab where love became a joke,
I dissected feelings, but they only choke.
With a scalpel of wit, I cut to the core,
Finding giggles where my heart felt sore.

Heartstrings tangled like a bad magic trick,
Poof! They vanished, but I'm still in the thick.
I analyzed tears like a science fair,
What's this? Just salt water, mixed with despair!

Each line of a love note, so close to the bone,
Comical findings in every sad tone.
Heartache's anatomy, a funny old sight,
Turns out it's just drama, dressed up for a fight.

Yet here in the shadows, I laugh and I fled,
With a heart made of pudding, I'm light as a thread.
So next time you wobble, don't take it to heart,
For laughter can mend even the worst kind of art.

## Anatomy of Remembrance

In the museum of memories, I stroll with delight,
Finding odd souvenirs from my past's blight.
A dancing banana in a tutu, oh dear,
Reminders of laughter amidst all the fear.

Photos with faces all scrunched in distress,
Chronicles penned in a comical mess.
There's mishap and mayhem mixed in the frame,
As I chuckle and snicker, it's all part of the game.

Each echo of laughter, a ghost of the day,
Tells tales of my trips that went the wrong way.
But oh, what a journey, with laughter to gain,
In heart's funny history, joy beats the pain.

So I raise a toast to the wild and absurd,
Finding humor in life like a jesting bird.
For every mistake that left a bitter taste,
There's a giggle, a chuckle, not one moment to waste.

## Emotional Alchemy

Mixing emotions like potions in a lab,
Turning tears to laughter, a whimsical jab.
With a dash of sunshine and a sprinkle of storm,
Alchemy of feelings takes a cheerful form.

Crafting joy from sorrow, oh what a tease,
Transmuting woes into giggles with ease.
Here's a potion for heartache, a sparkle from strife,
Behold! A new recipe for the comedy of life.

In my cauldron of feelings, I stir with delight,
Bubbling over with laughter, the pain takes flight.
Every frown gets a twist like a silly old rhyme,
Turning moments to magic, in rhythm and time.

So take out your flask, let the laughter ignite,
For the heart's greatest treasure is to find your own light.
In the dance of emotions, let's take to the air,
For a smile can transform even burdens to share.

## **Breathe Between the Cracks**

In the crevices of laughter, we find a twist,
Where humor hides in shadows, a cheeky mist.
Life's a jigsaw puzzle, missing a piece,
Yet we dance with joy, pretending it's fleece.

Giggling at the moments that don't quite fit,
Doing the cha-cha like it's all legit.
Cracks in the sidewalk, where dreams go to play,
We chase them like pigeons, come what may.

A sneeze turns into a riddle, oh what fun,
Laughter echoes loudly when we come undone.
Each slip is a treasure, every fall a delight,
Together we tumble, till the stars shine bright.

So breathe between cracks, let humor prevail,
In the chaos of life, let laughter set sail.
For the joy in the gaps is a playful embrace,
A tickled reminder, it's all a wild race.

## Melodies of a Torn Heart

A heartstring snaps but it sings a tune,
Like a cat in a blender, oh what a boon.
It's a serenade played by a broken string,
A laugh amidst tears, what joy they bring.

Dancing with misfortune, a tango of woe,
Twirl with the wrongs, let the good times flow.
A yodeling heart with a quirky refrain,
Every awkward note, a deliciously strange gain.

Chasing the notes from a heart that's in shreds,
We prank all the worries, ignore the dreads.
Each beat is a hiccup, a comic delight,
Making melodies shine in the dark of the night.

With laughter as rhythm, we find our rhythm,
Embracing the chaos, creating a prism.
So let's hum along to our silly ballet,
For even half-tunes can brighten the way.

## The Depths Beneath the Skin

Beneath my tough layer, a ticklish surprise,
A mélange of giggles that nobody spies.
Like a hidden stash of candy, it's sweet,
Just waiting for moments when my heart skips a beat.

Each wrinkle a whisper, each freckle a chat,
Where the mind plays tricks and the heart wears a hat.
A slip of the tongue, like a fish on a line,
Reveals all the treasures that glitter and shine.

So poke and prod gently, you might just find,
A goofy little secret, a whimsical mind.
In the depths of my layers, a soft, bouncy core,
Wobbling through life, and always wanting more.

With chuckles and grins as my trusty guides,
I wander these depths where laughter abides.
So come take a dive, with humor in tow,
Beneath the skin's surface, there's much more to show.

## Reverberations of a Hidden Scar

Whispers of laughter hang thick in the air,
A scar that reveals, like a crinkled old chair.
Every crease tells a story of plans gone awry,
Yet here we are giggling, oh me, oh my!

Bumps in the road that we chuckle and tease,
Launching our woes into a playful breeze.
Each scar is a badge, a ticklish old friend,
Reminding us gently that laughs never end.

With every mishap, a joke's underway,
Like slipping on marbles, we dance and play.
So gather your stories, the funny and stark,
And let them outshine every silly little mark.

In this tapestry woven with jests and with jibes,
We find all our strength in our humorous tribes.
For every scar shines with a giggle's embrace,
Transforming our trials into a whimsical space.

## **Pulses of Regret**

I tripped on my thoughts, oh what a scene,
My brain's a circus, my heart's a queen.
Regret does the limbo, oh so sly,
While I laugh it off, and just say, 'Why?'

A pizza too large, I took the slice,
Now I'm regretting, oh what a price.
I danced with dessert, oh sweet delight,
But my jeans whisper warnings late at night.

Dreams of grandeur, stacked like my fries,
Each one a rumor, your truth in disguise.
I chuckle and chuck, while plans hit the wall,
Life's a joke, and I'm just the clown at the ball.

Yet through the folly, lessons do tease,
Grinning at fate, I'll do as I please.
For every mishap just adds to my tale,
In this funny drama, I'll flourish, not fail.

# Fissures of the Forgotten

Dust bunnies gather, oh what a view,
Memories hiding, like long-lost shoes.
In the corners of life, they sit and they laugh,
While I chase my past like a wild giraffe.

The letter I wrote, but forgot to send,
Is like a bad joke that just won't end.
Lost in the shuffle, like socks in the wash,
Old ghostly giggles make my dreams posh.

A party so grand with no one in sight,
I danced with the shadows, what a fright!
Forgotten tunes played on an old radio,
Echoes of laughter, where did they go?

Yet among these fissures, a spark still glows,
Humor's the thread that nobody knows.
With a wink at the past, I'll move on with glee,
For the things that I treasure are just meant for me.

## **Veins of the Unseen**

Invisible threads weave through the air,
Tickling my thoughts, a mischievous bear.
In the shadows they dance, those quirks of the mind,
Poking and prodding, oh how they bind.

Whispers of worries float like a kite,
While I trip over hiccups, oh what a sight!
Unseen veins pulse with laughter and cheer,
As I juggle my dreams with a dash of fear.

A cat with a hat, a fish on a bike,
Reality bends like a comic delight.
The dull and the mundane blend in a twist,
As I laugh with my heart, I can't help but twist.

Yet hidden within these pranks life bestows,
Are treasures so funny, nobody knows.
I'll wear my quirks like a badge of pride,
For in the unseen, we find joy as our guide.

## **The Weight of Frailty**

A teetering tower of laundry awaits,
With socks that conspired to throw me through gates.
I giggle and tumble, embrace the misstep,
As gravity laughs, oh what a rep!

With each little crack in my grand facade,
Life leans in close, teasing me hard.
A fragile façade, like a glassy balloon,
Inflating my worries, oh what a tune!

A sneeze at the meeting, a watermelon slip,
I'll take my blunders with a hearty quip.
The weight of my frailty, a comedic show,
In the theater of life, let my laughter flow.

For within each fumble, a story unfolds,
Woven in humor, the future beholds.
I'll dance with my faults, wear them with cheer,
For in this mad journey, I'm forever sincere.

## The Depths of Dismay

In a puddle of thoughts, I found a shoe,
It fit like a glove, but it smelled like stew.
I slipped on a sock that was missing its mate,
And danced through the kitchen, oh isn't life great?

My refrigerator hums a sweet serenade,
To leftover pizza that's starting to fade.
A sandwich once proud, now a sad little flop,
I asked it for wisdom, it just told me to stop.

The cat on the counter, she eyes my last bite,
Waving her tail like she's ready to fight.
With a wink and a purr, she softens my frown,
As I laugh at the mess, she sprawls on the brown.

In the depths of my sorrow, I chuckle and grin,
For life's a grand circus, and I'm here to spin.
So let's toast with some juice, a toast that's quite bold,
To the chaos that tickles the heart and the soul!

## **Ribbons of Remorse**

Tangled in ribbons of what could have been,
I fumble my choices, a clumsy magician.
I laughed at the tub, oh the bubbles it made,
But slipped like a seal, how my dignity's frayed!

I wore mismatched socks, claimed it was a trend,
With polka dots dancing, I might just offend.
A friend sent me photos, mockery bright,
Yet I called it fine art, now isn't that right?

Banana peels waiting, a nasty surprise,
Trying to dance with them, oh how time flies!
Like a slip-n-slide hero, I feign to be cool,
While tripping and laughing, who needs a pool?

In ribbons of whoops, I embrace every fall,
For life is a party, and I'm having a ball.
So let's sip on the laughter, and snicker with glee,
For in every mishap, a bit of me's free!

## Etched in Silence

In the stillness of night, my thoughts start to play,
Like shadows on walls, in a jazz ballet.
I whispered my secrets to the cat on my lap,
He nodded in wisdom, then fell in a nap.

Pretzels in hand, I crunch and I chew,
The silence is golden, until I rue.
A sneeze from the couch sends the dog in a whirl,
As he chases his tail, oh what a grand twirl!

A fridge door swings wide, a monster unveiled,
My leftovers mutter, "You've really failed!"
Yet I smile at the chaos, and all it entails,
For laughter's the wind that fills all of my sails.

Etched in this silence, oh what a delight,
Like cartoonish sketches that twinkle at night.
So I'll toast to the quiet, with giggles and cheer,
For in the hush, life is quirky and clear!

## Chasms of the Heart

In chasms of giggles, I tumble and roll,
Feet tangled in humor, that's how I stroll.
I fell for a pun, it snapped like a drum,
And the laughter that followed, oh wasn't it fun?

My heart's a balloon, that's all full of air,
A crack in my laughter is nothing to bear.
With clown shoes to fill, I waddle around,
Each bounce a reminder that joy can be found.

I tripped on my dreams, they scattered like crumbs,
Each one a reminder, my spirit still hums.
In chasms of jest, I find little quirks,
That lighten my load, a true balm that works.

So I dance with my fumble, I twirl with my heart,
For laughter's a journey, an exquisite art.
In chasms of joy, may I wander and play,
For the smiles that blossom, keep darkness at bay!

## Echoes of the Heart's Divide

In love's wacky game we play,
The heart's a clown in bright display.
It trips on words, and stumbles too,
Yet laughs as it falls right back to you.

From joy to gloom, a swift ballet,
It dances on, come what may.
With every tick, the heart will shout,
Of silly doubts and lovers' pout.

But in a wink, it finds some cheer,
A giggle soft that winks so near.
For even when the tears do flow,
The heart knows well how to steal the show.

So here's a toast, to love's sweet jest,
Each twist a joy, each turn a test.
In laughter's grip, we'll surely find,
The heart's strange echoes, intertwined.

## Whispers Beneath the Surface

Beneath the calm, the fish do tease,
While hearts bounce round like bouncing bees.
They murmur sweet, but then they laugh,
At whispers lost in a watery path.

Each bubble forms a secret tale,
Of awkward winks and epic fails.
With fins that flap and tales that soar,
The heart's a jester, wanting more.

A splash, a grin, a joyous flip,
The heart can take such funny trips.
It wiggles here, it wiggles there,
For laughter lurks within the air.

So when you dive beneath the waves,
Remember joy is what it craves.
In whispers soft, let laughter reign,
The heart's rich tide, a sweet refrain.

## Chasms of the Silent Mind

In thoughts profound, a kangaroo,
Jumps through the gaps, oh what a view!
With silent screams that tickle loud,
The mind wears jokes, a funny shroud.

A maze of whims, a jester's play,
Thoughts spin and twirl in silly fray.
With every glance, the mind will jest,
It takes the guesswork as a test.

Oh what a ride in this tangled space,
With giggles bouncing at a rapid pace.
Through chasms deep, the chuckles tread,
A merry dance of thoughts misled.

So come, dear friend, let laughter bloom,
In silent nooks, dispel the gloom.
For in the mind, where echoes blend,
The joy of jest will never end.

## **Fragments of a Shattered Reflection**

In mirrors cracked, the smiles tease,
Reflecting back with funny ease.
Each shard a tale of quirks and grace,
Where laughter hides in every place.

With frayed edges of joy and woe,
The puzzle's fun, a goofy show.
Each piece of self, a comic twist,
In broken glass, what could be missed?

Wild colors clash in hapless cheer,
A fragmented dance that draws us near.
So smile at flaws, let's cheer the mess,
In every break lies happiness.

So gather round and laugh away,
These funny shards, we'll twist and sway.
For in the cracks, our hearts align,
A jesting heart that's truly fine.

## Inherited Scars

In the mirror, I see that frown,
A face that wears a clown's old gown.
Each wrinkle tells a funny tale,
Of falling flat, or missing mail.

My dad, he tripped on life's own cord,
Mom thought it best to wield a sword.
Our family jokes about the falls,
We giggle through our battle calls.

A scar from laughing far too hard,
A bruise from playing backyard bard.
We wear our marks with silly pride,
Like trophies from the goofball ride.

So here we stand, a merry band,
With stories stitched by fate's own hand.
Each scar a badge of humor's cheer,
Inherited joy that draws us near.

## **The Art of Breaking**

I try to dance, then break a plate,
It's all in fun, I celebrate!
With every slip, I lose my cool,
Artistry, yes, I'm a real fool.

My cat, she thinks she's quite the star,
She pounces hard, she runs afar.
But as she leaps, she hits the door,
Transforming us to laughter's floor.

In every prank, a joy revealed,
The art of chaos, well concealed.
With each mistake, the laughter flows,
As life unwinds, hilarity grows.

So here's to fun, to life's own flair,
With every tumble, let's all share.
The art of breaking brings delight,
Dance on, my friends, through day and night.

## **Threads of Longing**

I stitched a quilt of dreams and schemes,
With colors bright, all woven seams.
Yet every thread held some surprise,
Like tangled yarn, it twists and lies.

My heart's a loom, I yearn for joy,
But silly knots can be so coy.
Each pull and tug, a laugh erupts,
At what I made, the dread corrupts.

Through every patch of hope and fear,
I find the funny, I draw it near.
With each wild thread, my tale unfolds,
A tapestry in giggles told.

So when you see my quilt of dreams,
Know, it's more than what it seems.
A stitched-up joy, a playful feast,
Threads of longing turned to beast!

## Veils of Desolation

Behind the curtain, gloom takes flight,
Where shadows dance in the nightlight.
But lo, a joke breaks through the wall,
And laughter echoes down the hall.

In camouflage, despair takes shape,
Yet miming clowns can find escape.
Each veil a punchline masked in tears,
We chuckle through our greatest fears.

So while the world feels dark and grey,
We crack the jokes, we find our way.
Desolation wears a funny hat,
And laughter's where the heart is at.

So join the jest, embrace the jest,
For funny times, they are the best.
Through veils that hide the not so bright,
We dance and laugh, defying night.

## The Void Between Us

In a room apart, with snacks in hand,
I whisper jokes, but they don't land.
Your laugh's a ghost, floating through air,
While I'm stuck thinking, was it my hair?

Our chairs are distant, like planets in flight,
Orbiting thoughts in the dead of night.
I tell a pun; you snort like a hog,
Echoes of humor from the fog.

A dance of silence, a rhythm askew,
You trip on the punchline, fall out of view.
Here's to the gaps, the giggles we've shared,
Between our blunders, we know that we cared.

So let's bridge the void, with laughter and grace,
You in your seat, and I in my space.
In this comedy act, we are never apart,
Two hammy fools, joined at the heart.

**Tides of Transience**

Life ebbs and flows like a clumsy tide,
Crabs in my pockets, they refuse to hide.
They pinch my thoughts, as waves roll in,
While I'm marooned, trying to grin.

The sand slips through, like jokes on my tongue,
Each punchline fading, never yet flung.
An old beach ball, deflated and brown,
Reflects my hopes, half-heartedly down.

Seagulls squawk, with comedic flair,
Diving for fries, as I sit and stare.
The tide pulls back, leaves shells on the beach,
Like memories fading, just out of reach.

So I gather the laughter, the sun, and the breeze,
Splashing in humor, just trying to please.
Moments may drift, but with joy, I'll glide,
On the tides of transience, I'll take them in stride.

## Chronicles of the Broken

In the land of mishaps, where chaos reigns,
Broken umbrellas shed their pains.
I trip on a stone, but hey, it's all right—
Laughing, I twirl in the street—what a sight!

Once lost a shoe in the park today,
Old folks chuckled, saying, "Hip-hop ballet!"
With one on my foot, and the other a flop,
I skittered along, the town's latest prop.

My phone took a dive, right into my soup,
Messages floating like a foodie group.
Texting while cooking, what a grand plan,
I guess the soup got more fans than I can.

So here's to the snags, the shambles we weave,
In the book of my life, I choose to believe.
The chronicles tally, each mishap a gem,
Riding the waves of my own little whim.

## Reflection without a Pane

I stand by the mirror, but what do I see?
A clown in disguise, quite happy to be.
With socks that don't match and hair like a nest,
I dance with my shadow, just trying my best.

The glass is all fogged; I cannot behold,
Is it laughter, or wisdom, that's waiting to mold?
I scribble on surfaces, doodles and dreams,
A Picasso in coffee, or so it seems.

Friends laugh as I muddle, spill drinks on their clothes,
Like a slapstick routine, our humor just flows.
Reflections of joy, in an unfiltered light,
We celebrate blunders 'til the end of the night.

So here's to the moments, with or without a view,
With laughter, we'll conquer, create something new.
Life's a comedy show, it's on display,
No need for a mirror, just join in the play.

www.ingramcontent.com/pod-product-compliance
Lightning Source LLC
Chambersburg PA
CBHW060137230426
43661CB00003B/456